It's Our Government

Congress, the President, and the Courts

William Lefkowitz • **Richard Uhlich**

illustrated by P. L. McDonel

Consultant

Sherman Lewis, Ph.D.
Professor of Political Science
California State University
Hayward, California

Janus Books

a division of
Janus Book Publishers, Inc.
Hayward, California

Janus Government in Action Series

It's Our Government:
   Congress, the President, and the Courts

Government at Work:
   from City Hall to State Capitol

Acknowledgments

The authors and the publisher wish to thank the following people for their help in the development of the Janus *Government in Action* series:

Teachers
   Bernard Medeiros and Karen Taylor, Hayward (California) Unified School District; Jerrold Wisneki, Francis T. Maloney High School, Meriden, CT

City and County Officials, Middletown, CT
   Michael Cubeta, Mayor; Sergeant George Keithan, Police Department; Michael Kokoszka, Chief Clerk, Middlesex Superior Court; George Reif, Director of Planning and Zoning

Attorney at Law
   Verne A. Perry, Hayward, CA

Photo Sources
   We are grateful to all of the following for their help in obtaining photos:
   Nat Andriani, Ruth Day, Robin Dondero, Jane Fliesbach, Richard Geiger, Judith Gerrits, Wendy Green, Charles Millen, Linda Roberts, and Gerald Winn

Printed in the United States of America   678901234D-P098765

Contents

Introduction

Have you ever heard people say things like this?
   "They ought to fix these streets!"
   "They ought to stop crime!"
   "They ought to do something about high
   prices!"

Whom do these people mean by "they"?

These people mean the government. They mean that the government ought to fix the streets, stop crime, and bring down high prices.

But who or what is government? Is it a building, a place, a person, a group of people?

Government is all these things.

Government is the people who make, carry out, and apply our laws. Government is the places where these people work, and the things they use to do their work.

All the people who work for the government in the United States work for you! The places where they work and the things that they use all belong to you—and to the millions of other Americans.

That's because here in the United States we have a government "of the people, for the people, by the people."

Many Americans believe that ours is the fairest kind of government in the world today. But they also know we all have to work hard to keep it fair. To do that, we have to understand how our government works, and how we can take part in what it does.

You can understand how our government works.
You can take part in the work it does.
You can help make sure it works for you.
How? Read on and find out!

4

What Does Government Do?

Picture this...

It's 5 p.m. You're in a hurry to get home. You start to run. But when you get to the corner of Main Street, you stop dead in your tracks. Cars in the street stop dead too.

Why? Because the **traffic** light is out. No one knows when it is safe to go.*

Nobody moves. Everyone waits. People are getting upset.

What do you think would happen if you and the cars all made a wild dash at the same time?

Pow! Splat! Crunch! There'd be a real mess. Right?

---

*The words that appear in dark letters in a sentence are important words you should know.

5

Controls Traffic

Traffic is a big problem in any town or city. Someone has to do something to **control** it. That "someone" is government.

Think a moment. What does government usually do to keep cars and people from running into each other at street corners?

If you thought, "It puts up stop signs and traffic lights," you are right. Or you might have said, "It has a **police officer** on the corner." Either way, government helps to keep people safe by controlling traffic.

What are some other ways that government controls the traffic in your town or city?

Did you think of painted lines and crosswalks, **speed limits**, and traffic signs?

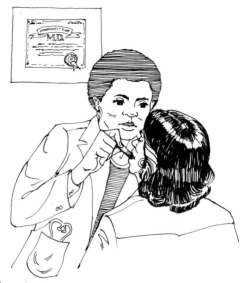

Picture this...

You have a really bad sore throat that won't go away. You can't sleep. You can't eat. You need to see a doctor.

OK. Somebody gives you the name of a doctor, and you go to see her.

But how can you find out if the doctor has the skills to take care of you?

Did you say that you can make sure she has a **license**?

Protects People

Doctors have to pass tests and get a license before they can treat people. They have to prove to the government that they have the skills to help people who are sick or hurt. This is one way the government helps to **protect** people.

Doctors aren't the only ones who have to get a license before they are allowed to do their job.

Take a look at the list below. Which of the people in the list do you think need a license?

1. Cooks
2. Dentists
3. Lawyers
4. Plumbers
5. Teachers
6. Clerks

Right. Dentists, lawyers, plumbers, and teachers need a license before they are allowed to work.

Picture this...

You live in an apartment house, and the house
is on fire. You're one of the lucky ones. You get
out quickly.

People on the upper floors are not so lucky. They
are trapped. There is no way out. The stairs are full
of smoke and fire. And the people are too high up
to jump.

Whom would you call to help save the people
trapped inside the building?

This is a job for the fire **department**. Right? It can
provide the help that's needed.

Provides Important Services

In most towns and cities, fire fighters work for the
government. They and the police help protect lives
and **property**. Protecting lives and property is just
one of the many important services that government
provides.

What are some other services that government
provides?

Did you think of schools, hospitals, and highways?

8

Picture this...

It's the last five seconds of a big game. The score is tied. Someone passes the ball to Ramirez.

Ramirez breaks loose and dribbles down the court. He's under the basket. He turns and leaps up to make a shot. It misses.

But wait a minute! Something's wrong! The **referee** is blowing her whistle.

What happened? The picture on this page tells the story. Why do you think the referee blew her whistle?

The referee saw player 32 hit Ramirez. That's against the rules. The referee is there to **enforce** the rules. She will let Ramirez take two free shots.

Makes and Enforces Laws

What do you think pro basketball would be like if there were no rules and no referees to enforce them?

You guessed it. There might be a lot of cheating and fighting.

The same is true in our daily lives. We all need rules to help us get along with each other.

Certain people in the government make those rules and call them **laws**. Other people in the government carry out and enforce those laws. That is, they make sure that we all **obey** the laws.

We have looked at four important things that government does. Government:
- controls traffic;
- protects people;
- provides important services; and
- makes and enforces laws.

Informed Citizen

An **informed citizen** knows a lot about his or her government. You are becoming an informed citizen by reading this book. See what you've learned so far.

Facts First

Each sentence below becomes a fact when you choose the best word or words to complete it.

1. Government helps control traffic by
   a. selling fewer cars.
   b. walking more.
   c. putting up traffic lights.
2. Before doctors or dentists can treat you, they have to ask the government for
   a. money.
   b. a license.
   c. tools.
3. Schools, hospitals, and fire departments are examples of some government
   a. laws.
   b. services.
   c. people.
4. The rules that government makes for us are called
   a. controls.
   b. licenses.
   c. laws.

Beyond the Facts

Here are some questions to think and talk about.

1. How does government make sure that people know how to drive safely?
2. Suppose government did not do this. What might happen?
3. Suppose there were no government at all. How might life be different for you?

Close to Home

Here is something you might like to do. It will help you see why government is really important to you.

Make two lists like the ones below. Add as many things to each list as you can think of.

Things Government Makes Me Do
1. Pay taxes
2. Stop at red lights

Things Government Does for Me
1. Puts out fires
2. Builds roads

Where Is Government Found?

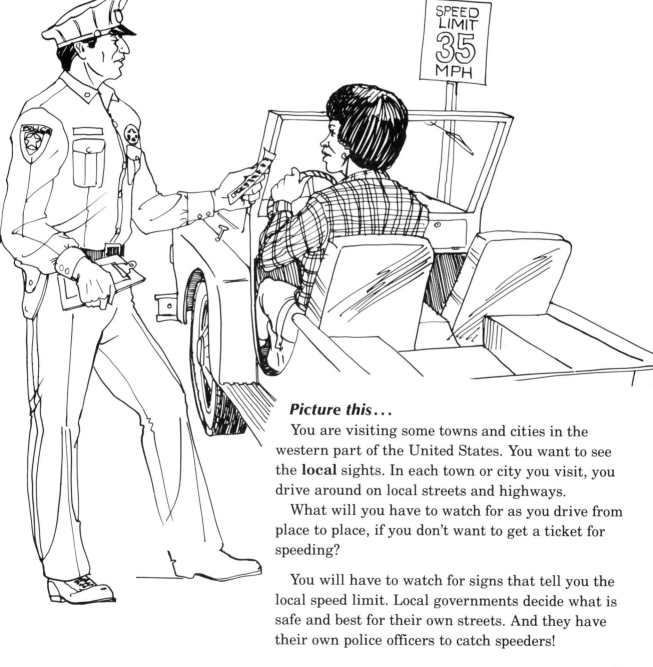

Picture this...

You are visiting some towns and cities in the western part of the United States. You want to see the **local** sights. In each town or city you visit, you drive around on local streets and highways.

What will you have to watch for as you drive from place to place, if you don't want to get a ticket for speeding?

You will have to watch for signs that tell you the local speed limit. Local governments decide what is safe and best for their own streets. And they have their own police officers to catch speeders!

Thousands of Local Governments

Look at the map. It shows seven towns and cities you might visit on a trip to the western part of the United States.

The map shows only seven places. But there are hundreds more in this part of the United States. And there are many thousands more in the rest of the country. Each town or city has some form of government to handle local matters.

Local government controls traffic. It gives people **permits** to build houses and other buildings. It sets up fire and police departments, schools, hospitals, and other important services. And it makes laws about local matters, such as where you can park a car.

You can usually find the people who run local government at town hall or city hall.

What is the name of your town or city?

Where do the people who run your local government meet?

12

Fifty State Governments

If you drove to all the towns and cities on the map, you would drive through seven states. All together, there are 50 states in the United States of America. Each of those 50 states has a state government.

A state government makes laws for all the people who live in that state. It also builds highways from one town or city to another. It tests drivers and gives out driver's licenses. It helps people who are out of work, and provides many other services.

State governments have offices all over the state. But the main offices are in the state **capital**. A state capital is a city where people meet to make the laws for a state.*

Two of the cities shown on the map are state capitals. Each of those cities has a star next to its name.

What is the capital of Texas? Of Colorado?

Austin is the capital of Texas. Denver is the capital of Colorado.

What is the name of your state? And what is its capital?

---

*The word *capitol*—with an *o*—means the building where lawmakers meet.

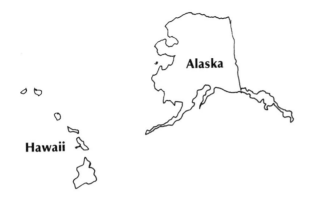

One United States of America

All the 50 states together make up one **nation** called the United States of America. *Nation* is another word for country.

The map shows the names of all 50 states. Find the name of your state. Which states are your neighbors?

Our Nation's Capital

Just as each state has a capital, so our nation has a capital. The nation's capital is Washington, D.C. That's where people meet to make **national** laws and do other business of the national government.

What *is* the business of the national government? For one thing, it prints and **coins** all the money we use.

The national government also makes laws that help people in one state do business with people in other states. It builds superhighways for fast travel from one end of the country to the other. And it deals with other countries.

Those are only a few of the many things the national government does.

14

Not Part of Any State

Find Washington, D.C., on the right side of the map. What state do you think Washington, D.C., is in?

It is not in any state! Washington, D.C., is the only city in the United States that is not part of a state.

How come? Because the people who set up the national government could not agree on which state the nation's capital should be in. So they decided it should not be part of any state.

Instead, the people said the nation's capital should sit on its own land, between the states of Maryland and Virginia. And that's still the way it is today.

15

A city worker trims plants in a city park. Which level of government does he work for?

Three Levels of Government

You may hear people say that the United States has three **levels** of government. What they mean is that we have local governments, state governments, and a national government.

Each level of government does different things.

- Local government takes care of things close to home.
- State government takes care of things that affect people all over the state.
- National government takes care of things that affect everyone in the country.

For example, which level of government do you think runs city parks?

Right, that's a job for local government.

Which level of government do you think gives people driver's licenses?

Right, that's a job for state government.

And which level of government do you think runs the army and navy?

Right again. The **armed forces** are run by the national government.

The rest of this book will be mostly about the national level of United States government.

16

Informed Citizen

Facts First

Choose the right word from the Word List to complete each sentence below.

Word List

state	Washington, D.C.
levels	local
capital	national

1. In the United States, we have three _____ of government.
2. Speed limits on town or city streets are set by _____ government.
3. You have to get your driver's license from your _____ government.
4. Money is printed and coined by the _____ government.
5. A city where people meet to make laws is called a _____ .
6. The capital of the United States is _____ .

Beyond the Facts

Here are some questions to think and talk about.

1. Who do you think should set speed limits on city streets—local, state, or national government? Why?
2. Who do you think should build and take care of highways that go all over the state—local, state, or national government? Why?
3. Who do you think should print and coin money—local, state, or national government? Why?

Close to Home

Here are some things you might like to do.

1. Find out what each level of government is up to these days. Read your local newspaper and listen to news programs on radio or TV. Look and listen for news stories about local, state, and national government. Talk about these news stories with classmates, family, and friends.
2. Make a scrapbook with different parts for local, state, and national news. Clip stories from newspapers and put them where they belong in the scrapbook.

Who Set Up Our Government?

Today you can travel from state to state with no problems. But it wasn't always that way. Back about 200 years ago, things were quite different.

Picture this...

The time is about 200 years ago.

You are living in the state of Maryland.

You want to travel to the city of Philadelphia in the state of Pennsylvania. You have to go there to buy some tea, gunpowder, and other things you need.

While you are in Philadelphia, you want to visit some friends. You pack your saddlebags with gifts of homemade soap and candles.

At the state line, where you leave Maryland and enter Pennsylvania, a **tax collector** stops you. He searches your saddlebags.

"You will have to pay a tax on these gifts," the tax collector says. "The money goes to the government of Pennsylvania."

"The government of Pennsylvania!" you shout. "Why should I pay money to the government of Pennsylvania?"

"Pay the money or turn back," the tax collector says.

You're really upset, but you pay the money and move on.

In Philadelphia, you go to a shop to buy some tea. You want to pay for the tea with Maryland money. But the shopkeeper says, "We only take Pennsylvania money here!" You walk out without your tea.

Could It Have Happened?

Do you think these things could have happened if you were living 200 years ago?

Yes, they could have. Because in those days there were only 13 states. Each state was like a separate country, with its own laws and money. And many states did not get along with each other.

There was a national government too. But it was very weak. It did not have the power to make the states obey its laws.

In 1787, however, things began to change.

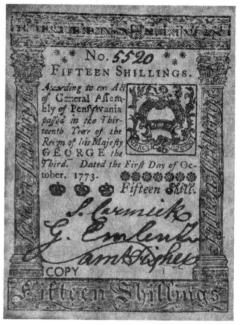

Pennsylvania money (1773)

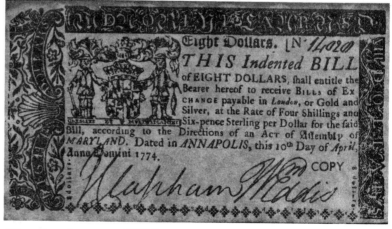

Maryland money (1774)

19

Important people from different states met in Philadelphia to plan a new national government. Can you name the two men whose faces are circled?

Meeting in Philadelphia

In 1787, the United States of America was only a few years old. And it wasn't very *united*!

That was only a few years after the states had won their freedom from England. The states had not yet learned how to form a strong, united nation.

Leaders in some of the states were worried that the new United States wouldn't last. They were afraid that each state would end up being a small country. Then stronger countries, such as England or Spain, might come in and take over each one.

Leaders Call Meeting

These leaders called for a meeting of important people from all the states. They wanted the people to make up a plan for a new national government—one that would help keep the states together and strong.

In May of 1787, **delegates** from 12 of the 13 states met in Philadelphia. A delegate is someone who is chosen by a group of people to speak for them at a meeting. Rhode Island refused to send any delegates. It didn't want any changes in the national government.

George Washington headed the meeting. Another famous person at the meeting was Benjamin Franklin.

Washington was a great leader. Franklin was very wise. It took all of Washington's strong leadership and Franklin's wisdom to get the delegates to agree on anything.

First Thirteen States

Philadelphia

20

The National Archives

Lots of Fighting

The meeting lasted from May to September—four long, hot months. The delegates talked and fought about what to do. Often, the talks became shouting matches.

Some of the delegates did not want a strong national government to rule over the states.

"We just fought a war to be free from English rule," said one of the delegates. "We don't want someone else now to tell us what we can and cannot do."

But another delegate said, "We need a strong national government to keep one state from making laws that hurt another state. And we need a strong national government to fight for us if we are attacked by England or Spain."

Suppose you were one of the delegates at the meeting. Which of the following would you vote for?

1. Strong state governments; weak national government
2. Strong national government; no state governments
3. Strong state governments; but even stronger national government

In the end, the delegates agreed to keep the strong state governments, but to make the national government even stronger than the states. This kind of government is called a **federal** government. Sometimes when we are talking about the national government, we call it the federal government.

Here is the opening of the Constitution and some of the first article.

Plan for Government

Once the delegates finally agreed on what to do, they wrote a plan for the new federal government. They called their plan the **Constitution of the United States**.

A constitution is a plan for government. It tells how the laws are to be made and carried out, and by whom.

A constitution may also tell what **powers** the government has. That is, it may tell what the government can and cannot do.

Some constitutions also tell what **rights** the people have. But the delegates didn't put a list of the people's rights in the U.S. Constitution. It wasn't added until later.

The Constitution of the United States has seven parts. Each part is called an **article**.

Informed Citizen

Facts First

Choose the best word or words to complete each sentence below.

1. Before 1787, the national government in America was
   a. strong.
   b. weak.
   c. unfair.
2. Delegates from different states met in Philadelphia to plan for a
   a. war with England.
   b. new state government.
   c. new national government.
3. The delegates agreed to
   a. do away with the national government.
   b. make the national government stronger.
   c. do away with state governments.
4. The delegates wrote a plan for government called a
   a. tax.
   b. court.
   c. constitution.
5. The delegates did not write anything in the Constitution about
   a. how government is set up.
   b. people's rights.
   c. how to add new laws.
6. Another name for the national government is the
   a. federal government.
   b. state government.
   c. local government.

Beyond the Facts

Here are some questions to think and talk about.

1. If you were going to send a delegate to speak for you at an important meeting, what kind of person would you want that delegate to be?
2. What do you think it takes to be a good leader of a group meeting?
3. What are some things the leader of a group must do to help members of the group reach some agreement? What must the members be willing to do?

Close to Home

Here is something you might like to do.

Write a constitution for your class or club. Talk over this idea with classmates or friends. Pick a leader to run the meeting. Talk about these things:

- Why might a constitution be helpful?
- What should the constitution tell?
- Who should decide what goes into the constitution?
- Who should write it?
- How will you make sure everyone obeys it?

After you read the next unit in this book, you will have a better idea of some of the things that you might put into your constitution.

How Is Power Kept in Check?

HOUSE RULES
1. NO LOUD MUSIC
2. NO PETS
3. NO PARTIES
4. NO VISITORS
5. LIGHTS OUT BY 10:00 PM
6. ROOMS MUST BE CLEANED DAILY.

Picture this...

You have been living in your own place for a few years. You're used to doing what you want to do, when you want to do it.

But your rent is high, and there has been a lot of crime lately. You're afraid of being robbed and beaten. So you're thinking of moving in with some other people. It will be cheaper and safer for you.

But those people want to set up rules about what you can and cannot do in the house. And they want one strong person or group to enforce the rules.

Would you be willing to give up some of your freedom in order to save money and feel safer?

Some delegates were afraid of losing their freedom.

Delegates Fear Super-Government

The delegates in Philadelphia had a similar question to answer. As long as the national government was weak, state governments had a lot of freedom. Many delegates were afraid that a strong national government would cut down on some of that freedom.

Other delegates were willing to give up some freedom in order to make things better between the states. And to get **protection** against attack.

But the delegates were afraid of giving too much power to any one person or group. That would be too much like the days when they were ruled by the king of England.

Power Split Three Ways

The delegates decided to **separate** the powers of the new federal government. That way, no one could ever have as much power over them as the king of England once had.

The delegates decided to split the powers of government among three groups of people.

- One group would make the laws.
- Another group would carry out and enforce the laws.
- A third group would hold trials, settle **disputes**, and decide if the laws were fair.

Three Branches

Today, we call each of the three groups a **branch** of government. There is a **legislative** branch, an **executive** branch, and a **judicial** branch.

The delegates wrote in the Constitution what they wanted each branch to do. Read on and find out what they had in mind.

This is the chamber, or big room, where the House of Representatives meets. The Senate meets in a similar chamber.

Here is what the Constitution says about the three branches. We have made the language easier to read.

Article 1: Legislative Branch

The legislative branch will make laws for the nation. The group that makes the laws will be called the **Congress**. The Congress will have two houses: a **House of Representatives**, and a **Senate**. The Congress will meet at least once a year.

The House of Representatives

To become a member of the House of Representatives, a person must be at least 25 years old. The person must have been a citizen of the United States for seven years, and must live in the state in which he or she is chosen.

Members are to be chosen from each of the states every second year. They are called **representatives**.

The Senate

To become a member of the Senate, a person must be at least 30 years old. The person must have been a citizen of the United States for nine years, and must live in the state in which he or she is chosen.

Each state may choose two members. The members will serve for six years. They are called **senators**.

Passing a Law

Any laws that the Congress wants must be approved and signed by the President of the United States. If the President does not approve and sign a law, the Congress may vote on it again. If **two-thirds** of those present in each house vote for the law, then it will become law without the President signing it.

Powers of the Congress

The Congress may:

1. Collect taxes and borrow money to pay the costs of government.
2. Control trade with other nations and between states.
3. Coin money.
4. Set up post offices.
5. Form armies and navies.
6. Declare war on other nations.

Checks on the Powers of the Congress

The Congress may not:

1. Take away the people's right to a speedy trial if they are arrested, unless the nation is in great danger.
2. Collect a tax on goods moved from one state to another.
3. Favor trade in one state over that in another.
4. Spend any money that has not been approved by law.

Article 2: Executive Branch

The executive branch will be headed by a President. The President will be **elected** by people from all the states for a four-year term. He or she must be at least 35 years old and must have been born in the United States.

Before taking over as President, the person must promise to "**preserve**, **protect**, and **defend** the Constitution of the United States."

Powers of the President

The President:

1. Is chief of the armed forces.
2. Is head of all departments that carry out and enforce U.S. laws.
3. May make **treaties** (agreements) with other nations.
4. May appoint people to high jobs in U.S. government.

Duties of the President

The President will:

1. Make sure that federal laws are carried out and enforced.
2. Report to the Congress about how the country is doing.
3. Suggest ways to solve the nation's problems.

Checks on the President's Powers

If found guilty of wrongdoing, the President may be removed from office by the Congress.

Article 3: Judicial Branch

The power to hear and decide **cases of law** belongs to the judicial branch. **Trials** for all **crimes** will be by **jury** (except for the trial of a President or other high government officer).

President Reagan reports to the Congress about how the country is doing.

United States House of Representatives

28

Informed Citizen

Facts First

Match each job on the left with the branch of government that does that job.

1. Carries out and enforces laws
2. Hear and decide cases of law
3. Makes federal laws

    a. The courts
    b. The Congress
    c. The President

4. Makes a law about the taxes people must pay
5. Makes sure that the law is obeyed
6. Hold the trials of people who are arrested for not paying their taxes

    d. The President
    e. The courts
    f. The Congress

Beyond the Facts

Here are some questions to think and talk about.

1. Why do you suppose people have to be a certain age before they can become members of the Congress or President of the United States?
2. The President must promise to "preserve, protect, and defend the Constitution of the United States." What do you think that promise means, and why is it necessary?
3. Do you think it is a good idea to separate the powers of government? Why or why not?

Close to Home

Here are some things you might like to do.

1. Are you working on a class or club constitution? If you are, you may want to list the powers of your officers the way the U.S. Constitution does. (See pages 27 and 28.)
2. Find out about the three branches of your local government.
   - Who makes local laws?
   - Who carries out and enforces those laws?
   - Who hears and decides cases of law?

What Are the People's Rights?

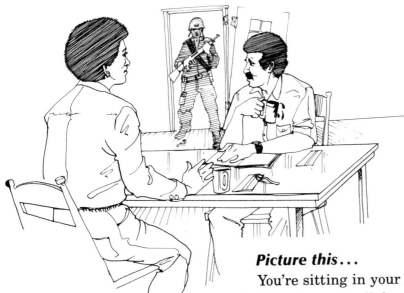

Picture this...

You're sitting in your kitchen with a friend, after looking for work all day.

"Sure is tough out there," says your friend. "I think the government is messing up real bad. That's why there are no jobs."

"That's what I think too," you say. "Fact is, that's just what I told someone today. I said..."

Suddenly your front door bangs open. A soldier rushes in.

"Hands up!" the soldier shouts. "You are **under arrest** for speaking against the government."

Do you think this could happen in the United States today?

No, it couldn't. Soldiers are not allowed to break into your home or arrest you for speaking against the government. You are protected from such things by the **Bill of Rights**. The Bill of Rights is a part of the Constitution.

Rights Were Added Later

At first, the Constitution didn't say enough about people's rights. That made a lot of Americans angry. They said such things as:

> There's nothing in this Constitution to protect us. The national government could throw us in jail for anything—and keep us there forever!

For a while, it looked as though many Americans would not accept the Constitution. If it was not accepted in at least nine of the states, it could not become law.

The delegates found an answer to the problem. What do you suppose they did?

Delegates Make a Promise

The delegates promised that as soon as the first Congress met, it would add a list of rights to the Constitution.

These rights would become the first **amendments** to the Constitution. An amendment is any law added to the Constitution after the Constitution has been accepted.

The promise of the delegates seemed to satisfy most people. They finally accepted the Constitution, even though it did not list their rights.

First Ten Amendments

In 1791, the people got their rights. Those rights were listed in the first ten amendments to the Constitution. These ten amendments became known as the Bill of Rights because they told about the people's rights.

The Bill of Rights was written almost 200 years ago. But it still protects you and all Americans from unfair government. How? Read on and find out.

All about Freedom

The First Amendment to the Constitution is all about freedom. It says that Americans have the right to four freedoms. These freedoms are described below.

First Amendment

1. **Freedom of Religion**

   The government may not force you to follow one **religion** or another. It may not stop you from following the religion of your choice.

2. **Freedom of Speech**

   The government may not keep you from making a **speech** about it or from saying what you think about it.

3. **Freedom of the Press**

   The government may not tell reporters and other members of the **press** what news they may or may not report.

4. **Freedom of Assembly**

   You have the right to **assemble** with other people and talk about the government, or to ask the government to do something, as long as your meeting is peaceful.

The First Amendment gives Americans the right to assemble and to speak out for what they want.

If You Are Arrested

The Fourth, Fifth, Sixth and Eighth Amendments are about being arrested. Here is how they protect you.

Fourth Amendment

The police must have a good reason to believe that you have broken a law before they may search your home or arrest you. Even then, unless they catch you breaking a law, they must first get a **warrant** from the courts. A warrant is a piece of paper that says the police may search your home or may arrest you.

Fifth Amendment

If you are arrested, you do not have to say anything that might make you seem **guilty**. Once you are on trial, you do not have to answer any question if you think your answer might make you seem guilty. If the court allows you to go free, you may not be arrested again for the same crime.

Sixth Amendment

If you are arrested, the police must tell you why they are arresting you. They must let you have a **lawyer**. And the government must give you a trial as soon as possible.

Eighth Amendment

Judges may not set **bail** at an amount too high for anyone to pay. Bail is money an accused person pays the court as a promise that he or she will appear for trial.

Judges may not set fines that are unreasonable. And they may not call for cruel or unusual punishment.

United Press International Photo

The man on the left has been arrested. What rights do you think he has, if any?

33

Five Other Amendments

Here are the other five amendments that are part of the Bill of Rights. Some of these amendments were very important to Americans at the time they were written. They may seem less important today. Which of the amendments do you think are still important?

Second Amendment

Since people may be called upon to help protect the country, the government may not keep people from owning guns.

Third Amendment

In time of peace, the government may not put soldiers in people's homes without permission from the people. If the government needs places for soldiers in wartime, it must pass a special law. The law would say that people must take soldiers into their homes.

Seventh Amendment

In court cases involving amounts of $20 or more, the people involved have the right to a trial by jury.

Ninth Amendment

Government may not take away other rights of the people just because those rights aren't listed in the Constitution.

Tenth Amendment

All those powers not listed in the Constitution as belonging to the federal government belong to the state governments or to the people.

If the army asked you to give these soldiers a place to stay, would you have to do it?

U.S. Army Photograph

34

Informed Citizen

Facts First

Choose the right word or words from the Word List to complete each sentence below.

Word List

amendments	Bill of Rights
search	arrested
freedoms	rights

1. At first, the Constitution did not say anything about the people's

   _____ .

2. Later, the first Congress added the first ten _____ to the Constitution.

3. The first ten amendments are also known as the _____ .

4. The First Amendment tells about four _____ .

5. The Fourth Amendment says the police must have a warrant before they may _____ your home.

6. The Fifth and Sixth Amendments tell what your rights are if you are

   _____ .

Beyond the Facts

Here are some questions to think and talk about.

1. Freedom of speech is one of the most important rights we have in the United States. Why?

2. Do you think freedom of speech means you can say anything you like, anytime, anywhere? Why or why not?

3. What do you think is a wise use of the right to free speech? What is not a wise use of that right?

Close to Home

Here are some things you might like to do.

1. If you are working on a constitution, add a bill of rights. First decide what rights class or club members ought to have. Then decide how many people in the class or the club must favor each right before it can become "law."

2. Start looking and listening for news stories about people's rights. Cut out the stories you see in newspapers and add them to your scrapbook. Talk about these stories with classmates, family, and friends.

What Makes a Democracy?

Picture this...

You belong to a club. The leader is big, strong, and smart. That's how he got to be leader, by outfighting and outsmarting everyone else. The leader tells you what to do, and you do it—or else!

Or else what? Well, maybe you have to pay a fine. Or maybe you get kicked out of the club. Or maybe you even get beaten up.

Are there clubs like this? Sure. There are clubs where the strongest person, or best fighter, or smartest person takes over.

Now picture this...

You belong to a different club. It is run by three people who are chosen each year by the members of the club.

This club has a written constitution. It tells what the leaders may and may not do.

Are there clubs like this? Sure.

Which of the two clubs would you rather belong to, the first or the second? Why?

Shared and Limited Power

Governments can be like those two clubs. In some governments, one person or one small group of people have all the power. They control the laws, the police, the army, and the courts.

Other governments are more like the second club. People choose their leaders and lawmakers. The power of those leaders and lawmakers is limited. And the people's rights are protected.

Is the government of the United States more like the first club or the second?

Our government is more like the second club.
- We choose our leaders and lawmakers.
- Their power is limited.
- Our rights are protected.

Our kind of government is called a **democracy**. *Democracy* means rule by the people.

Direct Democracy

There are two kinds of democracy. One is **direct** democracy. That's where people get together and make all the laws and decisions. For example, in some very small towns, all the voters meet in one place at one time. They make laws and choose leaders.

Representative Democracy

What if all the voters can't get together in one place at one time? Then we have a second kind of democracy, called representative democracy. A representative is any person who speaks for one or more other people.

Except in very small towns, we can't all get together to make our laws. So we send representatives to do it for us. The people in Congress are our representatives.

Making Democracy Work

The people who wrote the Constitution and the Bill of Rights made a good plan for a democracy. That plan has worked for about 200 years. In order for it to keep working, certain things have to keep on happening. Here are some of those things.

Free Elections

The government must hold **elections**. The main purpose of these elections is to give people the chance to choose leaders and lawmakers. The people must also be able to get rid of leaders or lawmakers who do not do a good job, or who misuse their power.

Freedom of Speech, Press, and Assembly

In order for democracy to work, people must be free to make choices. And in order to make *wise* choices, they must be well informed. People must be able to:

- find out what's going on in government;
- meet and talk about government;
- speak freely about the government; and
- bring about change in peaceful ways.

Majority Rule

The laws of the land must be acceptable to the **majority** of the people. *Majority* means more than half.

For example, for a new law to be passed by Congress, more than half of the people who vote that day in Congress must be in favor of the law.

Why do you think elections are important in a democracy?

Minority Rights

A nation like the United States has many different kinds of people and different groups of people. There are people of different races and religions, young and old, rich and poor, workers and owners, and so on.

In a democracy, the rights of all these people must be protected. The largest group, the majority, cannot take away the rights of any small group, or **minority**.

In a democracy, a minority group should have the same rights as the majority. What can a minority group do if it is not getting all its rights?

Shared Power

In a democracy, power must be shared. It cannot all be in the hands of one person or group. For example, in the United States, power is shared in two ways.

- Power is shared by three levels of government— local, state, and national.
- Power is shared by three branches of government—the Congress, the President, and the courts.

A Constitution

In a democracy, there must be a set of laws— a constitution—that tells what the government is supposed to do and what it may not do. The constitution must also tell how the laws are to be made, and how they are to be carried out and enforced.

39

Does the U.S. Pass the Test?

Now you know six important things that are needed to keep our democracy working. Decide if the United States has those things today. If you are not sure, try to find out by talking with classmates, friends, and relatives.

1. Can Americans choose their leaders and lawmakers?
   a. Yes
   b. No
   c. Not sure

2. Do Americans have freedom of speech, press, and assembly?
   a. Yes
   b. No
   c. Not sure

3. Does a majority of Congress have to be in favor of a law before it can become the law of the land?
   a. Yes
   b. No
   c. Not sure

4. Do minority groups have the same rights as the majority of Americans?
   a. Yes
   b. No
   c. Not sure

5. Is power shared by different levels and branches of government?
   a. Yes
   b. No
   c. Not sure

6. Does the United States have a written constitution?
   a. Yes
   b. No
   c. Not sure

7. Does the United States have the six important things needed to make democracy work?
   a. Yes
   b. No
   c. Not sure

Informed Citizen

Facts First

Choose the best word or words to complete each sentence below.

1. A government that is set up to help people rule themselves is called a
   a. constitution.
   b. city hall.
   c. democracy.
2. In order to let people choose leaders and lawmakers, the government must hold
   a. taxes.
   b. meetings.
   c. elections.
3. An important reason for freedom of speech, press, and assembly is so people can
   a. enjoy themselves.
   b. make wise choices.
   c. make a lot of money.
4. In a democracy, a new law cannot be passed unless it is approved by
   a. a minority of the lawmakers.
   b. an important leader.
   c. a majority of the lawmakers.
5. In a democracy, the powers and limits of government must be written down in a
   a. constitution.
   b. report.
   c. license.

Beyond the Facts

Here are some questions to think and talk about.

1. What are some things a government must do in order to be a democracy?
2. Do you think any of the following can be run like a democracy? Why or why not?
   - A family
   - A club
   - A class
   - A school

Close to Home

Here are some things you might like to do.

1. Think about the groups you belong to—such as your class, school, club, family, or place of work.
   - In which way is each group like a democracy?
   - In which way is each group not like a democracy?
   - Are there any changes you would like to see?
   - How could you help bring about those changes?
2. Suppose you wanted to help bring about changes in a group that you belong to. Prepare a short speech. Tell what you think is wrong and what changes you would like to see. Write or record the speech.

How Do People Get Elected?

Picture this...

You don't like the way things are going. Prices are too high. Too many people are out of work. Crime is spreading. You think it's high time somebody did something about all this.

Your friends think maybe that "somebody" should be you. They say you ought to be in the government. They think you ought to run for Congress.

At first, you just laugh at the idea. But then you start to think, "Maybe they are right. Maybe I ought to be in government."

"Hold on a minute," you say to yourself. "My friends would vote for me. My family would vote for me. But how could I get other people to vote for me?"

Do you know the answer to that question? Do you know how people get elected to public office? Read on and find out.

Political Parties Help

To win an election, a person usually needs the help of a **political party**. A political party is a group of people who work to get leaders and lawmakers elected to **public office**.

In the United States, the two biggest political parties are the Democrats and the Republicans. They each have thousands of members in every state.

Anyone Can Join

Anyone can be a member of a party. But most of the party's work is done by a small group of people.

These people want to help elect lawmakers who will make the kinds of laws the people think are needed. And they want to help elect leaders who will run the government the way the people think it should be run.

Both Democrats and Republicans believe in the Constitution and the Bill of Rights. But they often have different ideas about what needs to be done.

Different Ideas

One party may believe that government should spend more money to help people who are out of work. The other party might believe that government should help business first, because better business means more jobs.

Which party would you agree with:

1. The party that says help the people who are out of work?
2. The party that says help business first?

Which party does each animal stand for? The donkey stands for the Democrats. The elephant stands for the Republicans.

43

United Press International Photo

Becoming a Candidate

Let's say you decide to join a political party. So you find out what each party believes in. Then you choose the party whose beliefs seem closest to yours.

You become a member of that party, and you work in the small group of people who do most of the party's work.

Your friends know you belong to a political party, and they think you should be in the government. You think it over and decide you'd like to become a member of Congress.

You can try to get yourself elected, but that's usually pretty hard to do. A better way is to have your political party help you get elected.

First, you have to get your party to name you as its **candidate**. A candidate is a person who is running for public office.

But there may be other people in the party who also want to be the candidate. How would the party choose between you and the others? In one of two ways.

44

In 1980, Republicans met in Detroit to choose candidates for President and Vice-President. Democrats met in New York.

Political Conventions

Sometimes a party holds a **convention**. A convention is a big meeting.

The party chooses delegates to attend the meeting. The delegates listen to speeches by and about people who want to run for each public office. Finally, the delegates vote and choose the person they think will make the best candidate for each office.

Primary Elections

Sometimes a party holds a **primary election**. The party lists the names of all the possible candidates on a **ballot**. Then party members are given a chance to mark their choice on a copy of the ballot. Whoever gets the most votes becomes the party's candidate.

Winning Votes

Becoming your party's candidate is only the first step to getting elected. Next, you have to get people to vote for you on election day.

Candidates talk to people on the streets, at places of work, and in other public places. They make speeches at meetings and on radio and TV.

The candidates tell about the good things they have done, and what they will do if elected. They may also tell why they think they would do a better job than anyone else.

Party Workers Help

Party workers help the candidates win votes. They write and mail letters about the candidates. They put up posters, and give out balloons, buttons, and bumper stickers that tell something about the candidates.

Party workers also raise the money to pay for all this. Getting elected can cost thousands, even millions, of dollars!

Election Day

On the day that elections are held, voting machines are set up in schools, firehouses, and other places. Voters come and choose the candidate they want to see in each office.

Sometimes voters choose their own party's candidate. But sometimes they choose a candidate from another party who they think may do a better job. No one can tell whom they choose. Their vote is secret.

Finally the voting places close. The votes are counted. The candidate with the most votes wins.

United Press International Photo

Making posters for a candidate

Informed Citizen

Facts First

Decide if each statement below is true or false. If you think it is false, be ready to tell why you think so.

True or False

1. Political parties help people get elected.
2. The two biggest political parties in the United States are the Democrats and the Republicans.
3. A political convention is a big party for people who win elections.
4. Only party leaders can take part in choosing a party's candidates for public office.
5. A primary election is one in which people mark a ballot to show their choice for a party's candidate.
6. Party workers help raise the money that a candidate needs for posters, balloons, buttons, bumper stickers, and other things.
7. At election time, voters must vote for their party's candidate.
8. Voters must tell whom they voted for.

Beyond the Facts

Here are some questions to think and talk about.

1. Why do you suppose people want to be elected to a public office?
2. If someone doesn't have much money, could he or she still get elected? If so, how?
3. Not everyone has what it takes to be in government. But everyone can still help to shape government by doing work for a political party. What kind of work could *you* do? Which party would you want to work for?

Close to Home

Here is something you might like to do.

Form two parties in your own class. Decide what each party stands for. For example, one party might want strict rules, while the other party might want more freedom.

Decide what to call each party. Then get ready for an election, perhaps to choose a class president. First, each party chooses a candidate. Then each party helps its candidate win votes.

Finally, hold an election.

How Does Congress Work?

Picture this...

You ran for Congress and won! You are now one of the 435 members of the House of Representatives.

You live in Washington, D.C. Every morning, you start your busy day by watching the news on TV and checking the morning newspapers. You want to know what's going on in the world.

Most of your day is spent in meetings with other people. You have visits from some of the people from back home. You attend meetings with other representatives, helping to form new laws. You listen to arguments for and against new laws. You vote for some of the laws and against some others.

You spend a lot of time on the phone, getting and giving information. And you spend a lot of time reading and answering letters from the people back home.

Welcome to the Congress! How do you like your job so far?

Running Congress

Congress, you remember, is made up of two houses or parts. There is the House of Representatives, with 435 members. And there is the Senate, with 100 members. Together, the members of these two houses look at more than 20,000 **bills** a year!

A bill is an idea for a law. Each year, only a few hundred bills become laws.

How do the members of Congress decide which of the 20,000 bills to turn into laws? And how do they keep order in each of their houses? This unit and the next will tell you how.

Leaders Move Things Along

The Congress is like a school or business with many people and a big job to do. Someone has to decide who should do what and when. For example, someone has to decide who should study each of those 20,000 bills! These decisions are made by the leaders in Congress.

Top Leaders in House and Senate

Who is the top leader in the House of Representatives? A person called the **Speaker of the House** is. The Speaker runs meetings in the House chamber. That's the big room where members of the House come to **debate** and vote on bills. *Debate* means argue for or against something.

The Speaker also makes important decisions about who works on each bill. And if anything happens to the President and the Vice-President, the Speaker becomes the President of the United States.

The top leader in the Senate is the **majority leader**. This is a senator from the party that has the most members in the Senate.

Vice-President Bush (left) and Speaker of the House O'Neill listen to President Reagan in the House chamber.

United States House of Representatives

49

Majority and Minority Leaders

Some members of Congress are Democrats. Some are Republicans. Whichever party has more people in either house is called the **majority party** in that house. The party with fewer members is called the **minority party**.

In each house, there is a majority leader and a minority leader. These leaders help keep the work flowing smoothly between the members of their party. They also look out for their party's interests. For example, they try to get members who belong to their party to vote in favor of bills that the party wants.

Rules Must Be Followed

Part of the leaders' job is to make sure the rules of the House and the Senate are followed. Each house has its own set of rules. And each house may punish members who do not obey the rules. In fact, if two-thirds of either house thinks that a member has behaved very badly, they may vote to have that person removed from Congress.

Who says the House and the Senate may do these things? It is all written in the Constitution.

Office Workers

Hundreds of office workers help the representatives and the senators get their work done. There are assistants, secretaries, typists, messengers, and others. Besides the people who work for the whole House or Senate, each member of Congress has his or her own office **staff**.

Leaders, rules, and office workers—all help Congress do its job.

Coretta Scott King and two union leaders appear at a hearing. They give their opinions on a bill about jobs.

Committees Share the Load

With 20,000 bills to study every year, how can Congress possibly give each bill more than a moment's attention? The answer is by having **committees**.

A committee is a group of people who work together to find out something, to solve a problem, or to get a job done.

Committees Specialize

Most of the work done on bills in the Congress is done by committees. Each house has about 20 committees that **specialize** in certain kinds of laws. For example, both houses of Congress have committees that specialize in laws about **agriculture** (farming), about the armed services (army, navy, etc.), and about small businesses.

The members of these committees become experts about the needs of farmers, the armed services, the owners of small businesses, or whatever their specialty is. They write bills for laws that will help these groups. And they study bills written by others.

Committees Study and Vote

The committees gather information about each bill they are asked to study. They hold hearings (meetings) where they listen to the **opinions** of experts and concerned citizens. They debate the good things and the bad things in the bill.

Finally, the committees vote on the bills they have studied. The bills they pass are sent on to the House or Senate chambers for further debate and voting. Many of the 20,000 bills that are written each year never get past the committees.

Where the Ideas Come From

Only a senator or a representative can get a bill started in Congress. But they aren't the only ones who come up with the ideas for new laws. Where else do you think ideas come from?

From the President

Many of the ideas for bills that become laws come from the President's **program**. This program is a plan of things the government can do to help solve the nation's problems.

Presidents can't make laws. So they have to ask Congress to pass the laws that will make their programs work.

From Party Leaders

The members of Congress work closely with the leaders of their parties. Together they decide what to put into certain bills. They plan together how to get bills passed by the whole Congress.

From Special-Interest Groups

Farmers, bankers, workers, hikers—all have special interests. There are hundreds of such special-interest groups in the United States. They all want laws that will help meet their needs.

Many of these groups have special workers called **lobbyists**. These lobbyists spend much of their time talking to members of Congress. Sometimes they give the lawmakers ideas for new laws.

From Private Citizens

Members of Congress get many ideas from private citizens who write or visit them. Sometimes a bill is written to help just one person.

President Reagan prepares to send his ideas about government spending to Congress.

Informed Citizen

Facts First

Choose the right word or words from the Word List to complete each sentence below.

Word List

majority	Speaker
committees	majority leader
rules	program

1. The top leader in the House of Representatives is the _____ of the House.
2. The top leader in the Senate is the Senate's _____ .
3. The party that has the most members in the House or in the Senate is called the _____ party.
4. The Constitution says that each house of Congress may set up its own _____ .
5. Most of the work of writing and studying bills is done by _____ .
6. Many of the ideas for bills that become laws come from the President's _____ .

Beyond the Facts

Here are some questions to think and talk about.

1. Why do large groups need leaders and rules?
2. A committee will often do a better job than a larger group. Why?
3. Whom do you think members of Congress should listen to most and why?
   a. The President   c. Lobbyists
   b. Party leaders   d. People back home

Close to Home

Here is something you might like to do.

Find out who your representative and senators are.

Decide on something you would like to tell these people, or on something you would like to find out.

Form a few committees. Have each committee write a letter to a different representative or senator. Here is how you should address your letters:

For Senators
Senator _____
          Senator's Name
Senate Office Building
Washington, D.C. 20510

For Representatives
The Honorable _____
               Representative's Name
House Office Building
Washington, D.C. 20515

How Do Bills Become Laws?

Picture this...

You are in your home in Washington, D.C., ready to start another day in Congress. You are watching the news on TV. It shows that, in city after city, people are on the march. They want clean air and water. They want an end to **pollution**.

The people carry signs. They sing songs. They listen to speakers.

A few days later, the mail starts pouring in from the people you represent. The letter writers want laws that will help the country stop pollution.

What are you and the others in Congress going to do?

You're going to start writing some bills about pollution, right?

That's what happened back in the early 1970s. Many of the clean-air laws and anti-pollution laws we have now were written and passed then.

The Story of Your Bill

A bill is not a law. It is just a written plan for a law. A lot has to happen before that bill is passed.

Let's follow the steps that a bill has to go through to become a law. In fact, let's make it a bill that you, a member of the House of Representatives, want the Congress to pass.

Let's say that your bill calls for a law that will provide a certain amount of money to help schools teach about protecting the **environment**. *Environment* means the air around us, the woods, the rivers and lakes, and the animals that live in those places.

You Write Your Bill

First, you get all the information you can about what is happening to our environment, and about how schools might teach about the environment. Then you use this information to write a bill.

You Introduce Your Bill

You bring your bill to the desk of the Clerk of the House. That's where all House bills start out.

The Clerk of the House gives your bill a number. For example, the number might be **HR 9432**. (The **HR** stands for **H**ouse of **R**epresentatives.)

The Clerk gets your bill printed and sends copies to the Speaker of the House.

The Speaker Assigns Your Bill

The Speaker decides which committee your bill should go to for study. Since your bill is about helping schools, the Speaker sends it to the Education and Labor Committee.

A Subcommittee Studies Your Bill

The chairperson of the Education and Labor Committee gives your bill to a **subcommittee** called the House Subcommittee on Education. The subcommittee holds special hearings on the bill. It hears the opinions of teachers, students, scientists, artists, business people, and others.

Most of the people at the hearings are in favor of the bill. Some of them suggest a few changes. The members of the subcommittee write in the changes. Then they send your bill back to the chairperson of the Education and Labor Committee. They say that they think the bill should be passed.

The Committee Votes

The chairperson has the committee read your bill with the changes suggested by the subcommittee. The committee votes in favor of your bill.

A Time Is Chosen for House Vote

Once a committee approves a bill, it is usually sent to the Rules Committee. The Rules Committee then picks a time for the bill to be voted on by the House of Representatives. It also makes rules about how much debate will be allowed on the bill before the vote is taken.

However, on the first and third Mondays of every month, bills can go straight to the House. They don't have to go to the Rules Committee first. But these bills must get more votes than usual to pass.

You're sure of the votes; so you ask the committee to send your bill right to the House for voting.

This is where Congress meets—the Capitol Building in Washington, D.C. The House and Senate chambers and committee rooms are inside the building.

United Press International Photo

The House Debates and Votes

The time comes for the House to debate and vote on your bill. But there is very little debate, because most of the members are for it. The Speaker calls for a vote. The votes are counted.

Those in favor—289.

Those against—28.

Your bill has passed the House easily. But now it has to pass the Senate.

The Senate Passes Your Bill

Your bill goes through almost the same steps in the Senate. It starts with the Secretary of the Senate, who gives it a number that starts with an **S** (for Senate). Then it goes to a Senate leader who assigns it to a committee.

The committee studies the bill. Committee members make a few changes. Then they vote to approve the bill.

Since there is no Rules Committee in the Senate, the committee sends the bill to the majority leader of the Senate. The majority leader then calls for debate and a vote.

The Senate passes your bill 64-0.

House and Senate Make One Bill

Some members of the House and the Senate form a committee to agree on one final bill. They then send the final bill back to both houses for another vote.

Once again, your bill passes both houses. Now it's ready to go to the President of the United States.

The President Approves

The President reads your bill. He is concerned because the bill calls for spending more than he thinks should be spent. But he knows that most people in the United States would favor the bill. And he knows that it has won favor in the House and the Senate.

So the President decides to sign the bill. The moment he does, it becomes law.

President Can Veto Bill

If the President doesn't approve of a bill at all, he can **veto** it. That means he can send the bill back to Congress with a letter telling why he doesn't approve of it.

If Congress still wants the bill to become law, it has to take another vote in each house. But this time, two-thirds of the members have to favor the bill in order for it to pass. Then the bill can become law without going back to the President.

Pocket Veto

Here's something else that can happen. If a President keeps a bill for ten days without signing it, the bill automatically becomes law. But if Congress ends its work for the year before the ten days are up, the bill is automatically vetoed. This is called a **pocket veto**.

Based on a True Story

Back in 1970, Congress really did pass a law to help schools teach about the environment. The story of how it was passed is very similar to the story about your bill. We used the story to help you understand how bills become laws.

President Reagan signs a bill.

58

Informed Citizen

Facts First

Choose the best word or words to complete each sentence below.

1. A bill can be introduced in Congress only by
   a. the President.
   b. a member of Congress.
   c. a citizen.
2. House bills are assigned to committees by
   a. the Speaker of the House.
   b. the Vice-President.
   c. a clerk.
3. Committees often hold
   a. contests.
   b. hearings.
   c. trials.
4. Before a bill goes to the President, it has to pass in
   a. the Senate only.
   b. both the Senate and the House.
   c. the White House.
5. If a President doesn't like a bill, he or she can
   a. change it.
   b. tear it up.
   c. veto it (send it back to Congress).
6. If a President vetoes a bill, it may still become a law if Congress
   a. passes the bill by a two-thirds majority.
   b. holds the bill for ten days.
   c. sends it back to the President.

Beyond the Facts

Here are some questions to think and talk about.

1. It is not easy to get a law passed in Congress. Do you think this is good or bad for the country? Why?
2. What might happen if it were easy to get new laws passed?
3. Do you think the President should have the right to veto bills that a majority of Congress wants? Why or why not?

Close to Home

Here is something you might like to do.

Write bills for class or club rules.

First, form a few committees to study problems that your class or club faces. For example, you might have a Committee on Clean Up.

Choose a chairperson to run the meetings of each committee, and to make reports to the whole group.

Each committee writes a bill for a rule that will help solve a class or club problem. For example: The club will spend $20 to repaint the club room.

A Rules Committee can set up rules for debate and pick a time for voting.

What Does the President Do?

Picture this...

After many years in Congress, you ran for President and won. Now you are the President of the United States of America. You were **sworn** into office just a few weeks ago.

At this very moment, you are on your way to the House chamber. You are about to face Congress for the first time as President. You are going there to give a speech to the members of both houses.

This is your first chance to report to the lawmakers. You want to lay out your whole program for them. So you and your staff worked hard on your speech to make it just right.

The door to the House chamber opens as you reach it. Someone announces in a loud voice: "The President of the United States!"

Everyone in the room stands and turns to look at you. You walk to the platform. Millions of people are watching on TV. The world waits to hear your message. What will you tell them?

In 1980, President Sadat of Egypt visited President Carter. What do you suppose they talked about?

United Press International Photo

Three Jobs in One

Giving speeches is just one of the many things the President has to do. He really has three big jobs rolled into one. Let's see what each of these jobs is about.

Chief Executive

As chief executive, the President has to see that federal laws are carried out and enforced. He has to prepare a program to solve the nation's problems. And he has to prepare a **budget** to control government spending. A budget is a plan for spending money.

Chief of State

As chief of state, the President is in charge of our **relations** with other nations. He sees that we have agreements with other nations so that Americans can travel and do business there.

The President also sees that we have treaties with other nations. Treaties are agreements between nations in which they promise to help each other and not to attack each other.

Commander in Chief

About two million men and women serve in the armed forces of the United States. Their commander in chief is—you guessed it—the President.

The President can order the armed forces into action if we are attacked, or if he thinks American lives or interests are in danger overseas. He can also call out the troops anywhere in the United States to put down trouble or to help people in **emergencies**.

61

U.S. Navy Photograph

The top deck of the Russian ship is loaded with missiles. A U.S. Navy ship has come alongside.

One President's Power in Action

The two strongest nations in the world are the United States and Russia. The governments of the two nations often disagree about many things. But because they respect each other's strength, they have not tried to settle their differences by war.

Still, the people of the world become uneasy whenever the United States and Russia have strong disagreements. They know that both nations have enough power to destroy life on earth.

This was as true back in 1962 as it is today. At that time, John F. Kennedy was President of the United States. And Chairman Nikita Khrushchev was the leader of Russia.

Missiles in Cuba

The Russians had set up some of their **missiles** in Cuba, an island just 90 miles from Florida. Missiles are rocket bombs that can hit cities far away. The Russian missiles were pointed straight at the United States.

President Kennedy told Chairman Khrushchev to take the missiles out of Cuba. Khrushchev said "Nyet!"—which is Russian for "No!" Instead, the Russian leader sent out ships carrying more **weapons** for Cuba.

President Kennedy's Move

President Kennedy knew the next move was up to him. And if he made the wrong move, he might start a war that could destroy the world.

What was he to do? He did not want to let the Russians place more weapons in Cuba, so close to the United States. He wanted to stop them. But if he used too much force, the Russians might feel they had to fight. If he used too little force, the Russians might just laugh at him and go on doing as they pleased.

President Kennedy decided to take a chance. Acting as commander in chief, he sent some U.S. Navy ships into the waters around Cuba. He told the Russians that if their ships tried to pass through, they would be fired upon.

Chairman Khrushchev's Move

Now it was the Russian leader's turn to make a move. People all around the world waited to hear what Chairman Khrushchev would do. Would he order the Russian ships to sail on or turn back?

Finally, word came. Chairman Khrushchev ordered the Russian ships to turn around and head for home. No one fired a shot. Soon, the Russians began to remove their missiles from Cuba.

President Kennedy could have done nothing. Or he could have ordered planes to bomb the Russian ships and missiles—an act that might easily have led to war. Instead, he chose to show the power he was ready to use if he had to. This gave the Russians a chance to back away from a fight they really didn't want.

What would you have done if you were in President Kennedy's place?

United Press International Photo

Chairman Khrushchev and President Kennedy had a friendly meeting in 1961.

Replacing a President

What happens if a President dies? Leaves office? Is too sick to work?

- In 1963, just before Thanksgiving, President John F. Kennedy was shot to death. A few hours later, Vice-President Lyndon Johnson was sworn in as President.

- In August of 1974, President Richard Nixon gave up his job. He and some of his closest helpers were charged with trying to cover up their part in a break-in at Democratic party headquarters in Washington, D.C. Many people felt that President Nixon should no longer lead the nation.

   The President knew that he had lost the support of the people. He decided to quit, and Vice-President Gerald Ford became President.

- In March 1981, a man waiting in a crowd shot President Ronald Reagan. The bullet hit the President in the chest, not far from his heart. Would he live or die? If he lived, would he be able to carry on as President?

   The nation waited to see if Vice-President George Bush would have to step into the President's job. But President Reagan lived and soon went back to work.

When a President dies or can't hold office any longer, the Vice-President takes over to keep the nation running. The rule for this comes from Article 2 of the Constitution.

But what happens if the Vice-President also dies or can't serve? Who is next in line to take over?

Right, the Speaker of the House.

UPI/Bettmann Newsphotos

President Kennedy's casket is taken to the cemetery. Who replaced him as President?

64

Informed Citizen

Facts First

Choose the right word or words from the Word List to complete each sentence below.

Word List

armed forces   enforcing
missiles   ships
treaties   Vice-President
Speaker of the House

1. As chief executive, the President is in charge of carrying out and _____ the federal laws.
2. As chief of state, the President sees to it that we have agreements and _____ with other nations.
3. As commander in chief, the President is in charge of the nation's _____ .
4. President Kennedy wanted Russia to remove its _____ from Cuba.
5. President Kennedy ordered U.S. Navy _____ into the waters off Cuba.
6. If a President dies or leaves office, the job is taken over by the _____ .
7. If that person also dies or can't serve, the President's job goes next to the _____ .

Beyond the Facts

Here are some questions to think and talk about.

1. A lot of people would like to be President. Why do you think that's so? Would you?
2. Presidents seem to grow older very fast while they are in office. After four years in office, they sometimes look ten years older. Why do you think that happens?
3. What do you think it takes to be a good President?

Close to Home

Here is something you might like to do.

Watch newspapers and magazines for stories about the President. Cut them out. Put them in your scrapbook. Next to each story, write which of the President's three jobs the story is about—chief executive, chief of state, or commander in chief.

Also watch for stories about the President on TV. Talk to classmates, family, and friends about these stories. Maybe they saw the same ones. Discuss which of his jobs the President was doing in each story.

Who Works for the President?

Picture this...

Your day as President begins early this morning. You start by reading some reports.

The reports are about spring floods washing through five states. One report says that thousands of people have lost their homes. Other reports deal with food shortages, washed-out roads, and power failures.

At 8 a.m. you meet with your advisers. You ask them, "How many shelters are on hand? How much food and medicine is ready to go?"

Your advisers tell you all they can. But they can't tell you what to do. You alone have to decide.

You order troops at nearby army and air force bases to help save lives and property. You order the shipment of food, clothing, medicine, and other supplies.

Soon, thousands of federal troops and workers are carrying out your orders.

Millions of Troops and Workers

Close to two million people in the armed forces and three million government workers help the President carry out his work. But, of course, only a small number of these people work closely with the President.

White House Staff

The people who see and work with the President on a day-to-day basis are the members of the White House staff. These are special assistants, speech writers, secretaries, messengers, and others. Most of them work right in the White House, where the President lives and works.

Special Executive Groups

There are also groups of people who work closely with the President on certain kinds of problems. One of these groups is the **Office of Management and Budget (OMB)**. This group helps the President plan the federal government's budget.

Another important group is the National Security Council. This group helps the President find the best way to protect the United States.

Departments and Agencies

Most of the President's millions of helpers work for federal departments and **agencies**. There are about a dozen departments and 1200 agencies.

The difference between a department and an agency is this: A department may be involved with many kinds of problems; agencies usually specialize. For example, an agency called the **Internal Revenue Service (IRS)** collects taxes. And the **Federal Bureau of Investigation (FBI)** gathers information about people who break federal laws.

The White House in Washington, D.C.

United Press International Photo

Executive Departments

The list below names the 13 departments that help the chief executive. Some of these departments were started by our first President, George Washington. Others were added by later Presidents.

As you read over the list, ask yourself, "Does this department serve me in some way? If so, how?"

Department	What It Does
Agriculture	Helps farmers get fair prices and lends them money Teaches new ways to farm Inspects farm plants and animals for disease Manages national forests Manages food stamps
Commerce	Helps American business to grow and run smoothly Helps Americans do business with other countries Gathers important information about the population and the economy Sets standards for weights and measurements Gathers and reports information about the weather
Defense	Runs the armed forces Advises the President on military matters Plans for the nation's defense
Education	Gives money to public schools and colleges Sets up vocational training programs Sets up education programs for the handicapped Collects information about education and teaching Gives money for education research
Energy	Develops national energy plans and programs Works for energy conservation Carries on research into new kinds of energy Makes rules about the sale of electricity and natural gas between states

Department	What It Does
Health and Human Services	Makes sure foods and medicines are safe Gives money for research in health Helps people who are blind or disabled Runs the Social Security program Helps poor people pay for medical care
Housing and Urban Development	Helps rebuild old parts of towns and cities Helps cities clean up pollution Gives loans to build houses and businesses Helps poor people get housing
Interior	Runs the national parks Protects fish and wildlife Manages lands with minerals and forests Helps Native Americans Brings water to dry lands
Justice	Runs the FBI Runs federal prisons Goes to court for the government Takes care of immigration Enforces federal laws
Labor	Gathers job information and sets up training programs Pays unemployment benefits Sets up work safety rules Helps end labor strikes
State	Arranges treaties and agreements Gives out passports Advises the President on our relations with other countries Helps Americans travel and do business in other countries

Department	What It Does
Transportation	Builds federal highways Helps states build highways Makes rules for highway safety Helps railroads and public transportation lines Controls ship and airplane traffic Runs the Coast Guard during peace time
Treasury	Runs the IRS and pays the government's bills Prints and coins money Runs the Secret Service, which guards the President Enforces laws about firearms, tobacco, alcohol, and narcotics (hard drugs)

The Department Heads Form the Cabinet

The heads of all these departments are appointed by the President, with the Senate's approval. Their titles are Secretary of Agriculture, Secretary of Commerce, Secretary of Defense, and so on.

The President often calls on these department heads for their advice on important matters. Sometimes he meets with just one or two at a time. Sometimes he meets with all of them.

This group of department heads is sometimes called the President's cabinet.

President Reagan meets with his cabinet.

United Press International Photo

Informed Citizen

Facts First

On the left are nine jobs. On the right are the groups that do those jobs. Match each job with the group that does it.

1. Writes speeches for the President
2. Plans the federal budget
3. Helps protect the United States

4. Collects taxes
5. Gathers information about people who break federal laws
6. Guards the President

7. Helps farmers
8. Helps cities
9. Helps workers

a. Office of Management and Budget (OMB)
b. National Security Council
c. White House staff

d. Secret Service
e. Internal Revenue Service (IRS)
f. Federal Bureau of Investigation (FBI)

g. Department of Housing and Urban Development
h. Department of Labor
i. Department of Agriculture

Beyond the Facts

Here are some questions to think and talk about.

1. Which of the agencies and the departments affect your life in some way? How do they affect your life?
2. If you could work for any of the departments or agencies, which would you choose? Why?
3. Why do you think the President needs to have many advisers?

Close to Home

Here is something you might like to do.

Find out if there are any offices of federal departments and agencies in your community, town, or city. To find out, look in the telephone book under:

UNITED STATES
GOVERNMENT OFFICES

See if you can find any of the departments or agencies you have read about in this unit. Call or write one of them. Ask someone to visit your class to tell you about his or her work.

Who Pays for Government?

Picture this...

You are still the President of the United States. And you are sitting in your White House office, trying to work out some budget problems.

Here are some of the things you have to plan on paying for.

- Salaries for troops and government workers
- Ships, planes, and weapons
- Aid to the poor, the sick, and the jobless
- Aid to victims of floods and other disasters
- Building and repairing federal highways

This list is just a start. You're going to need more than $900 *billion* to pay all the bills. That's enough to buy a good motorcycle for every man, woman, and child in the United States!

Where are you going to get the money?

From the taxpayers, of course.

Income Taxes

Perhaps you or someone you know is a taxpayer. If you earn above a certain amount of money in any given year, you have to pay part of that money to the government. The part you pay is called an **income tax**.

Most of the federal government's **revenue** comes from income taxes. *Revenue* is money that the government collects in different ways.

IRS Collects

Congress decides how much tax money is needed each year, but the Internal Revenue Service (IRS) collects the money. How? By telling your employer to **deduct**, or take out, a certain amount of money from your pay every payday. Your employer must then send that money to the government.

At the end of the year, your employer must tell you how much you earned during the year and how much was deducted for income tax.

You Report

Then you have to fill out an income tax form. On this form you report how much you earned. You may list certain expenses. Then you figure out how much tax you owe for the year.

If your employer has deducted enough to cover what you owe, you won't have to pay any more income tax. If the deductions don't cover what you owe, you will have to pay the difference. If more was deducted than what you owe, you will get some money back from the government.

Every year, millions of Americans have to fill out an income tax form like this one.

Form **1040** Department of the Treasury—Internal Revenue Service **1981** (0)
U.S. Individual Income Tax Return

For the year January 1–December 31, 1981, or other tax year beginning , 1981, ending , 19 | OMB No. 1545–0074

Use IRS label. Otherwise, please print or type.	Your first name and initial (if joint return, also give spouse's name and initial) Last name	Your social security number
	Present home address (Number and street, including apartment number, or rural route)	Spouse's social security no.
	City, town or post office, State and ZIP code	Your occupation ▶

Presidential

Excise and Sales Taxes

You also pay taxes on many goods and services you buy. The amount charged for these taxes is anywhere from 2 to 12 cents on every dollar you spend.

Such taxes are called **excise** and sales taxes. *Excise* usually refers to taxes the federal government charges on goods and services. *Sales taxes* usually refers to taxes charged by state and local governments.

Excise Taxes

You have to pay federal excise taxes on many goods and services that the government thinks you don't absolutely need in order to live. For example, you pay an excise tax if you buy gas or cigarettes, and when you make a telephone call.

Sales Taxes

Many of the same things that are taxed by the federal government are also taxed by some state and local governments. But the state or local tax on these things is called a sales tax. State or local governments that have sales taxes may tax almost everything you buy. Most governments, however, do not tax food or medicine.

Stores and other businesses may include excise and sales taxes in the prices marked on things they sell. But usually they add the taxes to the prices later—when you pay for the things you buy. The stores and businesses send the tax money they collect to the local, state, and federal governments.

If you buy things this week, see if you can find out how much you are paying for excise or sales taxes.

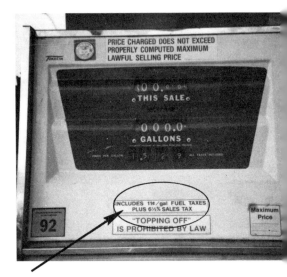

Federal, state, and local taxes are included in the price of gas.

Other Government Revenues

Besides the taxes you have learned about so far, governments have other ways to get the revenues they need. Here are some of those ways.

Social Security Tax

When people are old enough to retire from work, they may be able to collect Social Security benefits. The money to pay for this comes from the Social Security tax that is deducted from people's pay.

Import Taxes

The federal government charges **duties** or **import** taxes on goods that come here from other countries. For example, if you buy a camera that was made in another country, the price may include the amount charged for an import tax.

Fines and Licenses

All three levels of government collect fines from people who break laws. Industries pay federal fines for breaking safety and pollution laws. Drivers pay local fines for parking in no-parking areas.

Each level of government also sells licenses and permits. TV and radio stations get licenses from the federal government. Drivers, hunters, and doctors get licenses from their state governments. And businesses get permits from their local governments.

Property Taxes

State and local governments also get money from property taxes. These are taxes charged to the owners of land and buildings. Local governments get most of their money this way.

Did you ever pay a fine for parking where a sign told you not to?

Who Decides How Much?

The Constitution says that Congress "shall have the power to lay and collect taxes, duties,... and excises."

Congress and the President

All bills about federal taxes start in the House of Representatives. Then they go through all the steps you read about in unit 9 before they become laws.

But it is really the President who leads the way in deciding how much tax revenue will be needed. Once the President knows what he wants to do and how much everything will cost, he tries to get Congress to raise the amount of money needed.

The lawmakers don't always go along with what the President wants. Then they and the President have to work out their differences until they reach some agreement.

Congress May Borrow Money

If Congress can't raise enough tax money to pay all the bills, it may borrow money. But just like you and me, Congress has to pay **interest** when it borrows. Interest is the amount of extra money you have to pay back when you get a loan from a bank.

In recent years, the federal government has had to borrow a lot of money, and pay a lot of interest. Tax revenues have just not been enough to pay all the bills.

Of course, Congress could just raise everyone's taxes much higher than they've been. Why do you suppose the lawmakers haven't done this?

Right. Taxpayers might get really upset. Then they might not vote for those lawmakers when election time comes again.

Informed Citizen

Facts First

Decide if each statement below is true or false. If you think it is false, be ready to tell why you think so.

True or False

1. The government gets most of the money it needs from taxes the American people pay.
2. The Constitution gave the President the power to collect taxes.
3. Congress may borrow money.
4. The more money you earn, the less income tax you have to pay.
5. The job of collecting income taxes belongs to the courts.
6. Money for income taxes is deducted from people's paychecks.
7. Excise and sales taxes are taken out of people's paychecks too.
8. Charging property taxes on land and buildings is the main way local governments get their revenues.

Beyond the Facts

Here are some questions to think and talk about.

1. What kinds of taxes have you had to pay?
2. How do you feel about having to pay taxes?
3. People always complain about taxes. But we can't seem to do without them. Why do you think this is so?

Close to Home

Here are some things you might like to do.

1. Find out more about your state and local taxes. How much do you have to pay in sales taxes? What are the tolls on bridges and roads near you? How much does your state charge for a driver's license? For car registration?
2. One thing you'll do every time you start a new job is fill in a form for income tax deductions. It's called a Form W-4. Ask your teacher to get a copy and show you how to fill it in. You might also want to learn how to fill in a Form 1040. That's the form on which you report your earnings and deductions to the IRS.

What Do the Courts Do?

Picture this...

Tiny and Marie are returning from South America. They pick up their baggage and go through **customs**.

The customs **inspector** takes a quick look through Tiny's bag and tells him he can leave. But then he suddenly says to Tiny, "Wait a minute! Let me see your cap."

"My cap?" Tiny asks. "What for?"

"Just hand it over," says the inspector.

The inspector feels the inside and outside of the cap. He takes a small knife and slits the lining. Out fall several small bags of fine, white powder.

"How did they get in there?" Tiny asks with alarm.

"You must have picked up someone else's cap," says Marie.

"You both better come with me," says the inspector.

Later, Tiny and Marie are arrested for bringing **illegal** drugs into the country.

Criminal Cases

Are Tiny and Marie guilty or not guilty? That's for a court to decide. But they have been accused of committing a crime; so they will get a **criminal** trial.

A criminal trial is the kind you often see in movies or on TV. These trials usually take place in a criminal court, before a judge and a jury. However, a **defendant** may choose to have his or her case heard by a judge alone. A defendant is a person who is on trial.

The Jury's Job

There are usually 12 people on a jury. What do you think their job is?

The jury's job is to decide if the defendant is guilty or not guilty. The judge asks the jury to listen carefully to all the **evidence**, or facts, in the case. And he or she explains things the jury needs to know in order to make its decision.

The Verdict

At the end of the trial, the members of the jury go into another room and talk about the case. They try to decide if the defendant is guilty or not guilty. Their decision is called a **verdict**.

The jury returns to the courtroom and gives its verdict. If the verdict is "guilty," the judge decides what the defendant's punishment will be. If the verdict is "not guilty," the defendant goes free. If the members of the jury aren't able to agree on a verdict, the defendant may get another trial or may be set free.

Members of a jury are picked from the community.

Picture this...

Carol Ramos is a waitress. She bought a new car several months ago, with money she had saved from her tips.

Last month she was in a bad accident. The other driver was from another state and had no car insurance. The accident was his fault.

Carol is angry. Repairs on her car cost close to $1,000. In addition, she was hurt in the accident. She has another $1,000 in medical bills. Besides that, she couldn't work for several weeks. So she has lost the money she could have earned in tips.

Carol has asked the other driver to pay her bills and to make up for the money she has lost at work. The other driver refuses to pay a penny. What can Carol do?

Civil Cases

Carol can **sue** the other driver. That means she can take the other driver to court, and ask the court to order the other driver to pay her.

If Carol wins the case, the other driver may have to pay all her costs from the accident. He may also have to pay her lawyer's fees and court fees, plus something to make up for her lost income.

This kind of case is called a **civil** case and is tried in a civil court. Civil cases do not involve crimes like theft, robbery, or murder. They involve things like money, property, accidents, and **contracts**. A contract is an agreement to do business.

If only a small amount of money is involved, the case may be handled in a small claims court. Such courts usually handle cases that involve less than $1,500. The amount may be different in your state.

San Jose Mercury News

Local courts like this one are part of the state court system.

Federal and State Courts

Both the federal government and the state governments have courts. If a person is accused of breaking a federal law, he or she will be tried in a federal court.

For example, Tiny and Marie are accused of bringing illegal drugs into the country. That is against federal law. So Tiny and Marie will be tried in a federal criminal court.

If a case involves people from two or more states, it will also be tried in a federal court. For example, Carol is suing a driver from another state. So her case will be tried in a federal civil court.

Here are some other kinds of cases that would be tried in a federal court. A case is also tried in federal court if it involves:

- the United States government or any of its **officials**;
- members of the governments of other nations;
- the governments of two or more states;
- the government of a state and the government of another nation;
- a citizen of the United States and the government of another nation; or
- a citizen of the United States and a citizen of another nation.

All other cases are handled by state courts.

Suppose someone lives in Ashland, Oregon. And suppose that person wants to sue a plumber in Ashland for doing bad work in her house. Would the case go to a federal court or a state court?

Right. It would go to a state court.
Would it go to a criminal court or a civil court?

Right. It would go to a civil court.

Picture this...

The jury in Tiny and Marie's trial decides they are guilty. But Tiny and Marie still say they are not guilty. And their lawyer believes them.

What can Tiny and Marie do?

They can ask their lawyer to **appeal** the jury's verdict. That is, they can ask the judges of a higher court, a court of appeals, to review their case.

Courts of Appeals

Courts in the United States are arranged in a system of low, middle, and high courts. Traffic courts are on the low end. Trial courts, like the one where Tiny and Marie's case was heard, are in the middle. And courts of appeals are on the high end.

What all that means is this: A decision made in a trial court is not always final. A higher court may disagree with that decision. If it does, the higher court can **reverse**, or change, the verdict of the lower court.

Here's how a court of appeals works.

The judges from the court of appeals decide whether or not there seems to be a good reason for the appeal. If there does, the judges read a full report of the trial. They may also listen to the lawyers from both sides of the case.

Finally, the judges make a decision. They may decide to agree with the verdict of the trial court. Or they may reverse the decision of the trial court.

Let's look back at Tiny and Marie's case. If a court of appeals reverses the verdict of the trial court, Tiny and Marie may go free. Or they may be held for retrial.

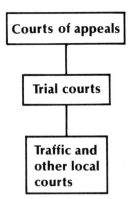

Informed Citizen

Facts First

Choose the right word from the Word List to complete each sentence below.

Word List

appeal	criminal
civil	state
reverse	verdict

1. People who are accused of committing crimes are tried in _____ courts.

2. Trials in which one person sues another person are held in _____ courts.

3. If a jury cannot agree on a _____, the defendant may get another trial or may go free.

4. If a defendant feels that he or she did not get a fair trial, he or she may _____ to a higher court.

5. Higher courts may _____ the verdicts of lower courts.

6. Both the federal government and the _____ governments have courts.

Beyond the Facts

Here are some questions to think and talk about.

1. Would you like to serve on a jury? Why or why not?

2. If you were on trial, would you want your case to be heard and decided by a jury or by a judge alone? Why?

3. What do you think might be some good reasons for appealing a case to a higher court?

Close to Home

Here are some things you might like to do.

1. Check local newspapers and TV news shows for stories about trials. Cut out the stories you find in newspapers and paste them in your scrapbook. Discuss the stories with classmates, family, and friends. Or pretend to be a TV news reporter and present the news to your class.

2. Find out what kinds of courts there are in your town, city, or area. Are there any federal courts? State courts? Do they have both criminal and civil trials? Is there a small claims court?

3. Visit one of the courts and see what you can learn about what the court does and how it works.

Why Is the Supreme Court Special?

Picture this...

It's the first Monday of October at 10 o'clock in the morning. The place is the United States Supreme Court in Washington, D.C. An officer of the Court bangs a **gavel** on a table top. At the sound of the gavel, everyone in the courtroom stands up.

Nine judges in long black robes enter the room from behind a red curtain. They are the nine **justices** of the Supreme Court.

The chief justice leads the way into the white marble courtroom. He walks to the tallest chair in the middle of nine black chairs at the high bench. The other justices take their places.

The officer of the Court calls, "Oyez! Oyez! Oyez!" These old words mean "Give me your attention!" The words are used to signal the start of the day's work.

The justices take their seats. Then everyone else sits. The Supreme Court is about to hear some appeals.

The Highest Court of Appeals

The Supreme Court is the highest court of appeals in the nation. No other court can reverse its decisions. In other words, it has the final say on any case of law.

Justices Pick Cases

Every year, thousands of people appeal their cases to the Supreme Court. But the nine justices can't deal with more than a few hundred cases a year. So they pick the ones that seem most important.

The justices listen to the lawyers from both sides of each case they agree to hear. And they study all the trial reports from those cases. They also see what their law books have to say about cases similar to the ones they are studying.

Then the justices meet together behind the locked doors of a guarded room. There they make decisions about the cases they have heard and studied.

Majority Decisions

Decisions are made by majority rule. That is, whatever a majority of the justices agrees on becomes the decision of the Supreme Court. So, all nine justices don't have to agree in order to have a decision. Only five or more must agree.

Every time the Supreme Court makes a decision, a justice who voted with the majority writes a paper to explain the decision. Sometimes, a justice who did not vote with the majority writes a paper to explain why he or she did not agree.

These papers help everyone understand the reasons for the decision. They also help lawyers and judges who may work on similar cases in the future.

United Press International Photo

From left to right are Justices Harry Blackmun, Thurgood Marshall, William Brennan, Warren Burger, Sandra Day O'Connor, Byron White, Lewis Powell, William Rehnquist, and John Paul Stevens. Warren Burger is the chief justice.

Guardian of the Constitution

Because it is the highest court in the nation, the Supreme Court has a special job to do. It watches over the highest law in the nation—the Constitution.

As **guardian** of the Constitution, the Supreme Court helps make sure that no one takes away our basic rights. And it settles disagreements about what the words in the Constitution mean.

The Supreme Court can also tell members of the government that their actions or laws are unconstitutional. That is, they can say that certain actions or laws go against the Constitution.

The Supreme Court can:

- tell a President or other elected leader that a certain action is unconstitutional;
- tell Congress or state and local lawmakers that a certain law is unconstitutional; and
- tell other courts that a certain decision is unconstitutional.

Let's look now at some of the decisions that the Supreme Court has made in recent years.

1954: Separate Schools

Up until 1954, some states had laws that said black children and white children could not go to the same schools. Many black parents thought that the schools for black children did not offer as good an education as the schools for white children did. So the parents wanted their children to be able to go to the same schools as white children went to.

The parents got a lawyer to help them. When the case came before the Supreme Court, the lawyer won.

The Court ruled that the state laws about separate schools were unconstitutional because they went against the Fourteenth Amendment to the Constitution. That amendment says that no state may deny any person "the equal protection of the laws."

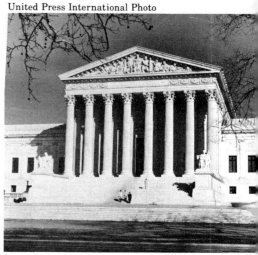

The Supreme Court Building in Washington, D.C.

1962: School Prayers

Up until 1962, most schools began their day with a prayer. Many parents did not approve of this. They said that prayers are part of religion, not education.

These parents said that the children in public schools were of different religions. So they did not think it was fair to make all children say the same prayer.

In 1963, the Supreme Court ruled that schools could not force students to say a prayer. The Court said forcing students to pray was unconstitutional because it denied one of the four freedoms given in the First Amendment—freedom of religion.

1981: The Draft

In certain times of danger to the nation, the Congress may pass a law to **draft** people into the armed forces. This means people have to serve, whether they want to or not.

In the past, only men have been drafted, not women. Some people thought that this was unconstitutional. They said that if men were to be drafted, women should be too.

But when the case came before the Supreme Court, the justices ruled that Congress could pass a law to draft men only. The Court said that Congress has that right because the Constitution gives Congress wide powers in matters of national defense.

Two Justices

The Supreme Court has become an important means for people to win and hold on to their rights in the United States. To do this well, the Court must represent all Americans.

But, for a long time, all of the justices were men. And all of them were white. There were no women. There were no members of minority groups.

First Black Justice

Thurgood Marshall was the first black person to become a Supreme Court justice. Marshall was the lawyer who won the case about separate schools for blacks.

President Kennedy made Marshall a federal judge. Later, President Johnson gave Marshall a job in the Justice Department. Then, when there was an opening on the Supreme Court in 1967, President Johnson appointed Marshall to the Court with the Senate's approval.

Thurgood Marshall

Sandra Day O'Connor

First Woman Justice

For a long time, many people have felt there should be women on the Court. In 1981, Sandra Day O'Connor became the first woman Supreme Court justice.

O'Connor had already had a long career in law. She had also been in the Arizona State Senate.

But when the time came for O'Connor to choose between working with laws or making laws, she chose working with laws. Soon she became a judge on the Arizona State Court of Appeals.

In 1981, there was an opening on the Supreme Court. President Reagan knew it was time to name a woman for the job. The woman he named was Sandra Day O'Connor. The Senate soon gave its approval.

Informed Citizen

Facts First

Decide if each statement below is true or false. If you think it is false, be ready to tell why you think so.

True or False

1. Presidents appoint Supreme Court justices to their jobs.
2. The justices study cases, listen to lawyers from both sides, study trial reports and law books, and then make their decisions.
3. The Supreme Court hears all the cases that people bring to it.
4. The Supreme Court is the highest court of appeals, and no other court can reverse its decisions.
5. The Supreme Court is the guardian of the Constitution.
6. The Supreme Court has no power over the President and the Congress.
7. The Supreme Court has done much to help protect people's basic rights.
8. To this day, there has never been a black justice or a woman justice.

Beyond the Facts

Here are some questions to think and talk about.

1. Why do you think the writers of the Constitution gave the Supreme Court the right to check on what the President and the Congress do?
2. The Supreme Court has often played a big role in protecting people's rights. Do you think that's an important role for the Court to play? Why?
3. A black and a woman now serve on the Supreme Court. Why is it important to have justices from different groups on the Court?

Close to Home

Here are some things you might like to do.

1. Watch for news about new Supreme Court decisions on TV and in the newspapers. Some of these decisions might affect your life or the lives of people you know. Discuss the decisions with your classmates, family, and friends.
2. Hold a Supreme Court Day in class. Choose people to play the justices, the lawyers, and the officer of the Court.

Is the Constitution Still Working?

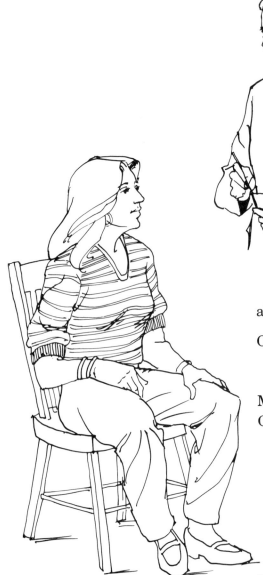

Picture this...

The police are about to question Mary Chase about stealing money from her boss.

OFFICER: Mary Chase, you are charged with stealing money. It is our duty to inform you of your rights before we begin to ask questions.

MARY: You mean I've got rights? Even in here?

OFFICER: First, you have the right to remain silent. Anything you say can and will be used against you in a court of law. Second, you have the right to talk to a lawyer and have the lawyer present with you while you are being questioned. Third, if you cannot afford to hire a lawyer, one will be appointed to be with you during any questioning, if you wish to have one present.

MARY: Well, I can't afford a lawyer, but I'd sure like one here when you question me.

OFFICER: OK, Ms. Chase. You will have to wait in a cell until the lawyer gets here.

The Miranda Case

Why did the police have to tell Mary Chase about her rights? Because of a Supreme Court decision made in 1966.

The case before the Supreme Court was about the rights of a man named Ernesto Miranda. The court based its decision on the Fifth and Sixth Amendments to the Constitution. Those are the amendments that tell about the rights of people who are arrested.

Here's what happened.

Ernesto Miranda

Didn't Know His Rights

Ernesto Miranda was arrested for a crime in Arizona in 1963. At the police station, no one told him about his constitutional rights. He didn't know he could have a lawyer. He didn't know he didn't have to say anything to the police.

Miranda just answered the police officers' questions. And after a few hours, he signed a **confession**.

Later, Miranda was given a lawyer and put on trial. His confession was used against him. He was found guilty and sent to prison.

Appeal Reaches Supreme Court

Miranda's lawyer thought that the confession wasn't fair. After all, Miranda didn't know his rights when he signed it. So the lawyer decided to appeal the verdict. By 1966, the case had made it all the way to the Supreme Court.

The Court agreed with the lawyer. The Court said Americans have the right to be told their constitutional rights if they are arrested. So now, when people are arrested, they must be told about their rights to remain silent and to have a lawyer.

In 1963, Martin Luther King, Jr., led a civil rights march in Washington, D.C. What do you suppose the marchers hoped to gain by marching in the nation's capital?

Picture this...

Late on the night of December 1, 1955, a black woman boards a city bus. She is going home from work. Her feet hurt, and she is tired. When she sees a seat in the middle of the bus, she takes it.

The bus moves on. At the next stop, more people get on. Then a lot more people get on at the next stop. The bus is crowded. People are standing in the aisle.

The bus driver calls back to the woman, "Get up and give your seat to the white person standing next to you."

The woman seems about to do it. But then she changes her mind. "No," she answers. "I'm not going to move." And she stays put.

The driver calls a police officer. And before Rosa Parks knows it, she's in jail.

Civil Rights

But what law was Rosa Parks accused of breaking? A city law saying blacks could sit only in the back of a bus. It was just one of many **segregation** laws that denied blacks their civil rights.

The segregation laws kept blacks from getting good jobs and living in nice homes. They separated blacks from whites in public places. And many of them made it hard for blacks to vote.

The arrest of Rosa Parks led to a Supreme Court decision that said such laws were unconstitutional. Here's how it all happened.

Bus Boycott

Most of the blacks in Montgomery, Alabama, where Rosa Parks lived, joined together under the leadership of Martin Luther King, Jr. For a year, they **boycotted** the city buses by not riding on them. The city lost a lot of money, but still the law didn't change.

Finally, late in 1956, Rosa Parks's case reached the Supreme Court. The Court ruled that segregation of blacks in public places was unconstitutional under the Fourteenth Amendment. This amendment guarantees all Americans "the equal protection of the laws."

Voters' Rights

The Supreme Court wasn't the only part of the government working to help blacks get their civil rights. Congress also took up the cause and passed many laws to end segregation.

One of those laws was the Voting Rights Act of 1965. It enforces the Fifteenth Amendment, which gives blacks the right to vote. Under the law, federal workers are sent to **register** blacks in places where local laws have kept them from signing up to vote.

The Equal Rights Amendment

There are other Americans besides blacks who feel they don't get all their rights. Among them are many women.

Women won the right to vote in 1920. The Nineteenth Amendment gave it to them. But so far, they haven't won equality with men in many other important ways. That's especially true when it comes to work.

Women now work at many jobs that once were only for men. But women are often paid less than men are paid. And they often don't get the top jobs.

NOW and ERA

A woman's group was formed in the 1960s to see what could be done to help women win more equality with men. That group is called the **N**ational **O**rganization for **W**omen (NOW).

NOW joined with other women's groups. Together they got Congress to pass the **E**qual **R**ights **A**mendment (ERA) in 1972. This amendment says that equal rights under the law can't be denied to women.

Not Approved

To become part of the Constitution, the ERA had to be approved by at least 38 states. That had to happen by June 30, 1982.

When that time came, only 35 states had approved the ERA. So the amendment did not become part of the Constitution.

In 1982, women's groups began working again for an equal rights amendment. The constitution protects their right to do this. Do you think they'll win next time? Why or why not?

San Francisco Examiner

Women's groups say they will continue to fight for women's rights and for an equal rights amendment.

94

Informed Citizen

Facts First

Choose the best words to complete each sentence below.

1. Because of the Miranda case, police must now tell an arrested person that he or she has the right to
   a. remain silent and have a lawyer.
   b. sign a confession and go to jail.
   c. appeal the case and go free.
2. Before the Rosa Parks case, blacks in some cities and towns had to
   a. stand in the aisle of a bus.
   b. ride in separate buses.
   c. sit in the back of a bus.
3. Segregation laws kept blacks from
   a. going to school.
   b. riding on buses.
   c. getting good jobs.
4. In Rosa Parks's case, the Supreme Court ruled that segregation was
   a. OK in public places.
   b. unconstitutional.
   c. guaranteed by the Fourteenth Amendment.
5. The purpose of the Equal Rights Amendment is to give
   a. blacks equal rights with whites.
   b. children equal rights with parents.
   c. women equal rights with men.

Beyond the Facts

Here are some things to think and talk about.

1. If you were arrested, what would be some of your rights, based on the Miranda case?
2. What other groups besides blacks and women think they don't have equal rights? Do you agree with them?
3. Do you think the Constitution is still working? Why or why not?

Close to Home

Here are some things you might like to do.

1. Review what you have learned. Form several teams. Have each team read again one or two units of this book. Then have each team tell the class the main ideas in the unit or units it read.
2. After the review, choose up sides for a game of Informed Citizen. Have the teacher or someone else ask questions from the Facts First exercise at the end of each unit. Or make up questions to ask. Make up your own rules for how to play the game and for choosing a winner.

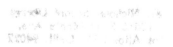

Index